2023 APPROACH TO SOCIAL MEDIA MANAGEMENT

A SIMPLE GUIDE TO STARTING SOCIAL MEDIA MANAGEMENT

By Agatha Simeon

2023

APPROACH TO SOCIAL

MEDIA MANAGEMENT

A Simple Guide To Starting Social Media Management.

By Agatha Simeon

BECOME A DISTRIBUTOR

Are you interested in making the idea of social media management grow higher?

You can make a living by becoming a distributor of **"2023 APPROACH TO SOCIAL MEDIA MANAGEMENT"**

By Agatha Simeon

CONTACT;

nellygstar@gmail.com

agathasimeon8@gmail.com

08062470547, 08130874904

RECOMMENDATION

"Dominating Online Entertainment The board: Your Manual for Turning into an Expert in under One Month!" is a must-peruse for anybody seeking to succeed in the powerful field of virtual entertainment the executives. This thorough aide, masterfully composed by a carefully prepared industry proficient, gives a bit by bit guide to furnish perusers with the abilities and information expected to flourish in the consistently developing computerized scene.

The book starts by establishing major areas of strength for a, presenting the idea of web-based entertainment the board and its importance in this day and age. It investigates the advancement of online entertainment, featuring key patterns and arising stages that are forming the business. This extensive comprehension makes way for perusers to dig further into the complexities of the field.

One of the book's assets lies in its pragmatic methodology. It not just acclimates perusers with famous web-based entertainment stages yet in addition gives important bits of knowledge into their socioeconomics, functionalities, and best practices. Perusers are directed on choosing the right stages for their clients or business, guaranteeing a designated and viable virtual entertainment presence.

Expanding upon this establishment, the book then, at that point, plunges into creating a successful online entertainment methodology. It assists perusers with recognizing their interest group, direct statistical surveying, and foster purchaser personas. By stressing content creation, curation, and dispersion, perusers figure out how to enrapture their crowd and improve commitment. The book additionally covers local area the executives best practices and development techniques to encourage flourishing web-based networks.

What separates this book is its accentuation on viable instruments and methods. It acquaints perusers with fundamental virtual entertainment the board apparatuses and shows how to use their functionalities for proficient booking, investigation observing, and commitment. Furthermore, the book offers significant guidance on remaining refreshed with new devices and patterns, guaranteeing perusers are prepared to adjust to the consistently changing web-based entertainment scene.

The composing style is connecting with and open, making complex ideas and procedures straightforward. Every part is very much organized, giving clear goals and rundowns, alongside functional activities and contextual investigations that support the growing experience. The incorporation of significant hints and genuine models further upgrades the book's worth.

"Dominating Virtual Entertainment The board" is a thorough aide that engages perusers to become capable web-based entertainment directors in a limited capacity to focus time. It outfits them with the fundamental abilities, information, and techniques to certainly explore the difficulties of the business. Whether you're a fledgling or hoping to upgrade your current abilities, this book is a significant asset that certifications to raise your online entertainment the board game.

With its quality substance and commonsense methodology, "Dominating Online Entertainment The executives" is ready to be a hit on the lookout. It can possibly change hopeful web-based entertainment administrators into skillful experts, and I strongly prescribe it to anybody looking for progress in this speedy computerized field.

READER'S ENDORSEMENT

I'm more than happy to earnestly support SIMEON AGATHA as a social media manager. Having had the delight of working intimately with SIMEON AGATHA on various tasks, I can unhesitatingly say that her aptitude and commitment is unrivaled. She has a profound comprehension of social media management stages and patterns, easily making an interpretation of that information into significant techniques that drive commitment and results. Their capacity to create convincing substance and curate a credible brand voice separates them from the rest. With her in charge, you can believe that social media presence will flourish, having an enduring impact on

ENDORSEMENT 2:

It gives me extraordinary delight to embrace SIMEON AGATHA as social media expert. SIMEON AGATHA is an expert of her specialty, reliably conveying exceptional outcomes in the steadily developing universe of social media. Her essential outlook, joined with a creative methodology, guarantees that each mission she contact is a resonating achievement. She has a remarkable capacity to comprehend and interface with interest groups, making custom-made content that resounds profoundly. With her uncommon local area the executives abilities and development systems, she will without a doubt hoist your social media image higher than ever. In the event that you're searching for a social media director who can change your business, she is the unequivocal decision.

DEDICATION

This book is devoted to every one of the hopeful social media administrators who have an enthusiasm for making significant associations and igniting discussions in the immense domain of social media media management

To the tireless students, the ones who are focused on keeping steady over the always changing patterns and stages, this book is for you. May its pages act as an aide, outfitting you with the information, abilities, and techniques to explore the thrilling and dynamic universe of social media management.

I commit this book to the trailblazers, the ones who won't hesitate to examine and consider some fresh possibilities. May it move you to release your inventiveness, empowering you to make drawing in happy and construct flourishing networks.

To the specialists and information devotees, this book is a recognition for your insightful personalities and careful preparation. May it engage you to foster compelling social media methodologies, upheld by experiences and measurements, that drive quantifiable outcomes.

Finally, this devotion is for the visionaries and achievers. May this book be your venturing stone towards understanding your objectives and desires in the social media management. Keep in mind, with devotion, persistence, and the information acquired inside these pages, you have the ability to have an effect and flourish in this thrilling field.

This book is devoted to you — the social media managers of tomorrow. Embrace the excursion, embrace the conceivable outcomes, and influence the advanced circle.

ACKNOWLEDGEMENT

Composing this book has been an ongoing source of both pain and joy, and I might want to offer my genuine thanks to every one of the people who have upheld and added to its creation.

Above all else, I stretch out my genuine thanks to the endless social media managers and industry experts who have liberally shared their bits of knowledge, encounters, and ability. Your important information has molded the substance of this book and has been instrumental in giving functional, certifiable viewpoints.

I might want to communicate my most profound appreciation to my manager, whose sharp eye and meticulousness have refined the composition into its last structure. Your direction and skill have been priceless all through the whole interaction.

At long last, I might want to offer my most profound thanks to the pursuers. It is for you that this book was composed. Your excitement and hunger for information rouse me to keep sharing significant bits of knowledge and assets.

To every one of those referenced above and to the endless other people who play had an impact, huge or little, in the formation of this book, I broaden my sincere much obliged. Your help and commitments have made this excursion both satisfying and fulfilling.

Much thanks to all of you.

FORWARD

In the time of computerized network and social media, the job of social media manager has arisen as a fundamental part in the outcome of organizations and people the same. As we wind up submerged in this present reality where online presence can represent the moment of truth an association, the interest for talented experts who can explore the steadily changing scene of social media management..

From the beginning, this book submerges perusers in the underpinnings of social media management. It fastidiously covers the basics, giving a strong comprehension of the job, its development, and the special difficulties looked by experts in this powerful field. By establishing perusers in the basics, the creator lays the preparation for the extraordinary excursion that lies ahead.

What separates this book is its common sense. Every section is painstakingly created to convey noteworthy experiences and substantial methodologies that can be promptly executed. Through a mix of true models, contextual investigations, and functional activities, perusers are furnished with the devices important to succeed in the specialty of web-based entertainment the board. Whether it's characterizing ideal interest groups, making convincing substance, or examining measurements for consistent improvement, this book investigates every possibility.

Besides, this guide goes past the nuts and bolts, plunging into cutting edge systems and arising patterns that are molding the social media scene. From force to be reckoned with showcasing to saddling the force of client produced content, pursuers will acquire a top to bottom comprehension of state of the art strategies that can impel their social media presence higher than ever.

The creator's skill radiates through each page, as they offer bits of knowledge into the subtleties of various social media stages. From Facebook to Instagram, Twitter to LinkedIn, every stage is analyzed, furnishing pursuers with fundamental information on socioeconomics, best practices, and methodologies for amplifying commitment. By engaging peruses to arrive at informed conclusions about stage choice and advancement, this book furnishes them with the certainty to explore the assorted computerized biological system.

Along these lines, dear pursuer, I welcome you to leave on this excursion of revelation and development. Get ready to open your true capacity, extend your range of abilities, and raise your social media management ability. By embracing the information and bits of knowledge inside these pages, you will be well en route to turning into a well equipped social media chief, ready for outcome in a computerized world that blossoms with association, commitment, and development.

Here's to your excursion of taking over social media management.

AGATHA NNENNA SIMEON

TABLE OF CONTENTS

DISCOVERING THE ROLES AND RESPONSIBILITIES OF A SOCIAL MEDIA MANAGER.

EXPLORING THE BENEFITS AND CHALLENGES OF A CAREER IN SOCIAL MEDIA MANAGEMENT.

BENEFITS OF A CAREER IN SOCIAL MEDIA MANAGEMENT

Chapter Two

THE EVOLUTION OF SOCIAL MEDIA

- **<u>Examining the impact of social media on businesses and individuals</u>**
- HIGHLIGHTING KEY TRENDS AND EMERGING PLATFORMS IN THE SOCIAL MEDIA LANDSCAPE.

SECTION TWO

Chapter Three

BUILDING THE FOUNDATION

Understanding the role of strategies in social media management.

- How to use ChatGPT to generate ideas for your content
- Copywriting
- Content publishing
- Exploring target audience, and the use of key performance indicators (KPIs)
- The use of KPIs and metrics

IMPLEMENTING THE GOALS AND OBJECTIVES OF SOCIAL MEDIA MANAGEMENT

SECTION THREE

Chapter Four

- **THE USE OF ADVERTISEMENT**

Chapter Five

FACE BOOK AND INSTAGRAM ADS

Twitter influencing

- LinkedIn building

INTRODUCTION

In the advanced age, social media has changed the manner in which we convey, associate, and direct business. With billions of individuals overall connecting on different social media, it has turned into a strong power that fundamentally influences the economy. Inside this scene, the job of social media management has arisen as a vital part of hierarchical achievement and development.

Social media management includes a scope of systems and procedures focused on really using social media process to accomplish business goals. From building brand mindfulness and drawing in with clients to driving site traffic and creating prospective customers, the effect of social media on the economy can't be undervalued.

In the present profoundly serious market, organizations that disregard the force of social media do as such at their own danger. Social media stages give unrivaled open doors to organizations to reach and interface with their main interest group on a worldwide scale. Through essential substance creation, local area the executives, and information driven bits of knowledge, virtual entertainment administrators can use these stages to make significant connections, upgrade brand notoriety, and drive substantial business results.

As the economy keeps on developing in a computerized course, the significance of social media management turns out to be progressively clear. By tackling the force of social media, associations can adjust to the steadily changing shopper scene, gain an upper hand, and encourage reasonable development. In this book, we investigate the major standards and high level systems of social media management, furnishing pursuers with the information and abilities important to flourish in the present economy.

SECTION ONE

Understanding Social Media Management

Chapter One

WHAT SOCIAL MEDIA MANAGEMENT IS.

Social media has revolutionized the way we connect, communicate, and share information in the digital age. It refers to online platforms and applications that enable users to create, share, and engage with content in a social and interactive manner. These platforms facilitate the exchange of user-generated content, including text, images, videos, and links, among a vast network of individuals and communities.

At its core, social media is about fostering connections and building relationships. It provides a space for people to express themselves, share their thoughts and experiences, and engage in conversations with others who share similar interests or goals. Social media platforms have transformed the way we stay connected with friends and family, discover new ideas, and engage with brands and businesses.

Social media platforms come in various forms, catering to different types of interactions and content sharing. Some of the most popular social media platforms include Facebook, Instagram, Twitter, LinkedIn, YouTube, and Snapchat. Each platform has its own unique features and functionalities, targeting different demographics and catering to specific purposes.

Social media has become a fundamental part of our daily lives, with billions of people actively engaging on these platforms. It has reshaped the way we consume news, gather information, and make purchasing decisions. Social media has also democratized content creation, allowing individuals and businesses alike to amplify their voices and reach a global audience without the need for traditional gatekeepers.

Businesses have recognized the power of social media as a marketing and customer engagement tool. It provides a direct line of communication between brands and their target audience, enabling real-time interactions and personalized experiences. Social media platforms offer businesses the opportunity to showcase their products or services, build brand awareness, and cultivate a loyal customer base through targeted advertising, influencer partnerships, and engaging content strategies.

While social media offers numerous benefits, it also presents challenges and considerations. Privacy concerns, online harassment, and the spread of misinformation are some of the issues that arise within the social media landscape. Responsible social media management involves safeguarding user privacy, promoting digital literacy, and fostering a safe and inclusive online environment.

THE IMPORTANCE OF SOCIAL MEDIA MANAGEMENT IN TODAY'S LANDSCAPE

In today's interconnected world, social media has become an integral part of our daily lives. From sharing personal experiences to discovering new products and services, social media platforms have revolutionized the way we connect, communicate, and consume information. Within this digital landscape, the role of social media management has emerged as a critical component for individuals and businesses aiming to thrive in the modern era. In this chapter, we will explore the importance of social media management in today's landscape and how it can significantly impact personal branding, business growth, and customer engagement.

Personal Branding and Online Presence

In an increasingly digital world, personal branding has gained significant importance. Social media platforms serve as powerful tools for individuals to shape their online identity, showcase their expertise, and build a network of connections. Effective social media management enables individuals to curate their online presence, highlight their skills, and establish themselves as thought leaders in their respective fields.

By strategically crafting and sharing relevant content, social media managers can help individuals enhance their visibility, expand their network, and open doors to new opportunities. Furthermore, social media management allows for real-time engagement with followers and facilitates meaningful interactions, fostering a sense of authenticity and trust. Whether it's maintaining a consistent posting schedule, responding promptly to comments, or leveraging storytelling techniques, social media managers play a crucial role in helping individuals shape and maintain their personal brand in today's digital landscape.

Business Growth and Customer Engagement

For businesses, social media management has become a cornerstone of success in the digital age.

Social media platforms offer unparalleled opportunities to connect directly with target audiences, build brand awareness, and drive customer engagement. With billions of users active on various social media platforms, businesses that neglect the power of social media do so at their own detriment.

Effective social media management allows businesses to develop a strong online presence, showcasing their products or services, and conveying their brand's unique value proposition. Social media managers employ strategic content creation, community management, and data-driven insights to captivate audiences, foster brand loyalty, and drive conversions.

Moreover, social media management enables businesses to stay in tune with customer preferences, market trends, and competitor activities. By actively monitoring conversations, analyzing engagement metrics, and leveraging social listening tools, social media managers gain valuable insights into customer sentiment, enabling businesses to adapt their strategies and offerings accordingly. This customer-centric approach not only enhances customer satisfaction but also helps businesses stay agile and competitive in a rapidly evolving marketplace.

Targeted Marketing and Advertising

One of the key advantages of social media management lies in its ability to enable targeted marketing and advertising. Social media platforms offer robust targeting options that allow businesses to reach their ideal audience with precision. Through effective social media management, businesses can create tailored campaigns based on demographics, interests, behaviors, and even specific locations.

Social media managers play a crucial role in understanding the target audience and developing strategies that resonate with them. They leverage data and analytics to identify key insights, such as peak engagement times, preferred content formats, and trending topics. By leveraging this information, social media managers can optimize marketing efforts and ensure that messaging reaches the right people at the right time.

Additionally, social media platforms provide various advertising formats, including sponsored posts, display ads, and influencer collaborations. Social media managers possess the expertise to identify the most effective advertising channels, optimize ad campaigns for maximum reach and engagement, and measure the return on investment. Their ability to navigate the intricacies of social media advertising ensures that businesses allocate their resources effectively, yielding tangible results and maximizing their marketing budgets.

Crisis Management and Reputation Building

In the computerized age, a brand's standing can be essentially affected by how it oversees emergencies and answers client criticism. Web-based entertainment the board assumes a crucial part in proactively tending to client concerns, overseeing possible emergencies, and protecting a brand's standing.

Online entertainment supervisors go about as the main line of guard, checking web-based entertainment stages for client criticism, audits, and remarks. By instantly answering requests, objections, or negative criticism, they can relieve issues before they raise and transform them into amazing open doors for goal and improvement. Virtual entertainment directors grasp the significance of straightforwardness, sympathy, and successful correspondence, guaranteeing that clients feel appreciated and esteemed.

Besides, online entertainment the board works with the development of a positive brand picture and local area commitment. Web-based entertainment supervisors can foster substance systems that feature a brand's qualities, exhibit its social obligation drives, and encourage a feeling of local area among devotees. By supporting legitimate connections, web-based entertainment chiefs can transform clients into brand advocates, intensifying positive opinion and building long haul unwaveringness.

In the midst of emergency, virtual entertainment supervisors are instrumental in overseeing correspondence and tending to public worries. They utilize emergency the executives techniques, like opportune and straightforward updates, facilitated informing, and proactive commitment, to limit reputational harm and keep up with entrust with partners. In the computerized age, a brand's standing can be essentially affected by how it oversees emergencies and answers client criticism. Web-based entertainment the board assumes a crucial part in proactively tending to client concerns, overseeing possible emergencies, and protecting a brand's standing.

Online entertainment supervisors go about as the main line of guard, checking web-based entertainment stages for client criticism, audits, and remarks. By instantly answering requests, objections, or negative criticism, they can relieve issues before they raise and transform them into amazing open doors for goal and improvement. Virtual entertainment directors grasp the significance of straightforwardness, sympathy, and successful correspondence, guaranteeing that clients feel appreciated and esteemed.

Besides, online entertainment the board works with the development of a positive brand picture and local area commitment. Web-based entertainment supervisors can foster substance systems that feature a brand's qualities, exhibit its social obligation drives, and encourage a feeling of local area among devotees. By supporting legitimate connections, web-based entertainment chiefs can transform clients into brand advocates, intensifying positive opinion and building long haul unwaveringness.

In the midst of emergency, virtual entertainment supervisors are instrumental in overseeing correspondence and tending to public worries. They utilize emergency the executives techniques, like opportune and straightforward updates, facilitated informing, and proactive commitment, to limit reputational harm and keep up with entrust with partners. In the computerized age, a brand's standing can be essentially affected by how it oversees emergencies and answers client criticism. Web-based entertainment the board assumes a crucial part in proactively tending to client concerns, overseeing possible emergencies, and protecting a brand's standing.

Online entertainment supervisors go about as the main line of guard, checking web-based entertainment stages for client criticism, audits, and remarks. By instantly answering requests, objections, or negative criticism, they can relieve issues before they raise and transform them into amazing open doors for goal and improvement. Virtual entertainment directors grasp the significance of straightforwardness, sympathy, and successful correspondence, guaranteeing that clients feel appreciated and esteemed.

Besides, online entertainment the board works with the development of a positive brand picture and local area commitment. Web-based entertainment supervisors can foster substance systems that feature a brand's qualities, exhibit its social obligation drives, and encourage a feeling of local area among devotees. By supporting legitimate connections, web-based entertainment chiefs can transform clients into brand advocates, intensifying positive opinion and building long haul unwaveringness.

In the midst of emergency, virtual entertainment supervisors are instrumental in overseeing correspondence and tending to public worries. They utilize emergency the executives techniques, like opportune and straightforward updates, facilitated informing, and proactive commitment, to limit reputational harm and keep up with entrust with partners.

DISCOVERING THE ROLES AND RESPONSIBILITIES OF A SOCIAL MEDIA MANAGER.

Content Creation: The social media manager is responsible for developing engaging and relevant content that aligns with the brand's voice and objectives.

Community Management: They interact with the audience, respond to comments and messages, and nurture relationships with followers to foster engagement and build brand loyalty.

Social Media Strategy: Developing and executing a comprehensive social media strategy that aligns with the brand's goals, target audience, and industry trends.

Analytics and Reporting: Monitoring social media metrics, analyzing data, and providing insights to optimize performance and inform decision-making.

Advertising Campaigns: Planning and executing targeted advertising campaigns across various social media platforms to maximize reach and achieve marketing objectives.

Influencer Partnerships: Identifying and collaborating with relevant influencers to amplify brand visibility and tap into their engaged audience.

Social Listening: Monitoring conversations, trends, and mentions related to the brand, industry, or competitors, to gain insights and identify opportunities.

Brand Management: Ensuring brand consistency and maintaining a positive brand image by monitoring mentions, handling customer feedback, and resolving issues promptly.

Stay Current with Trends: Staying up to date with the latest social media trends, algorithm changes, and emerging platforms to implement innovative strategies and tactics.

Cross-Functional Collaboration: Collaborating with other departments, such as marketing, PR, and customer service, to ensure cohesive messaging and a unified brand presence across channels.

These roles require a combination of creativity, strategic thinking, strong communication skills, and a deep understanding of the target audience and social media platforms. A skilled social media manager can effectively leverage these responsibilities to drive brand awareness, engagement, and business growth in the digital landscape.

EXPLORING THE BENEFITS AND CHALLENGES OF A CAREER IN SOCIAL MEDIA MANAGEMENT.

BENEFITS OF A CAREER IN SOCIAL MEDIA MANAGEMENT

Creativity and Expression: Social media management allows individuals to express their creativity through content creation and storytelling.

Impact and Influence: The ability to make a meaningful impact by shaping brands, connecting with audiences, and driving business growth.

Continuous Learning: The dynamic nature of social media keeps professionals constantly learning and adapting to new trends, tools, and strategies.

Flexibility and Remote Work Opportunities: Many social media management roles offer flexibility in terms of work hours and the possibility of remote work.

Networking and Collaboration: Opportunities to connect with professionals in various industries, build relationships, and collaborate on innovative campaigns.

CHALLENGES OF A CAREER IN SOCIAL MEDIA MANAGEMENT

Fast-Paced and Ever-Changing: Social media management requires keeping up with rapid platform updates, algorithm changes, and emerging trends.

High Expectations and Pressure: The pressure to deliver engaging content, meet performance targets, and handle customer concerns in real-time.

Managing Multiple Platforms: Juggling multiple social media platforms, each with its own unique requirements and audience, can be challenging.

Reputation Management and Crisis Response: Navigating potential reputation crises and addressing negative feedback while maintaining a positive brand image.

Time-Intensive and Always-On: Social media management often involves round-the-clock monitoring, responding to messages and comments, and managing content schedules.

A career in social media management offers exciting opportunities for growth, creativity, and influence, but it also demands adaptability, resilience, and a proactive approach to stay ahead in this rapidly evolving field.

Chapter Two

THE EVOLUTION OF SOCIAL MEDIA

<u>Examining the impact of social media on businesses and individuals</u>

Social media has had a transformative impact on both businesses and individuals, revolutionizing the way we connect, communicate, and engage in the digital age. For businesses, social media has become an essential tool for brand building, customer engagement, and driving growth. Individuals, on the other hand, have experienced a shift in personal branding, networking, and self-expression.

Social media has enabled businesses to reach a global audience, irrespective of their size or location. It has leveled the playing field, providing equal opportunities for startups, small businesses, and established brands to showcase their products or services. Through strategic social media management, businesses can create an authentic online presence, engage with customers in real-time, and foster brand loyalty.

The impact of social media on businesses extends beyond marketing and customer engagement. It has facilitated the rise of influencer marketing, where individuals with large social media followings can collaborate with brands and drive product awareness and sales. Social media platforms have also introduced e-commerce features, allowing businesses to sell products directly to their social media followers, thereby reducing friction in the purchase journey.

For individuals, social media has provided a platform for personal branding, networking, and self-expression. It allows individuals to curate their online identities, showcase their skills, and establish themselves as thought leaders in their respective fields. Social media has become a powerful tool for networking and building professional relationships, opening doors to new opportunities and collaborations.

However, the impact of social media is not without its challenges. Privacy concerns, online harassment, and the spread of misinformation are issues that individuals and businesses must navigate. Social media has created a need for digital literacy, critical thinking, and responsible usage to ensure a safe and positive online environment.

In summary, the impact of social media on businesses and individuals cannot be overstated. It has transformed the way businesses operate, market their products, and engage with customers. Social media has also empowered individuals to shape their personal brands, network with like-minded individuals, and showcase their talents and expertise. While social media brings immense opportunities, it also requires careful management, responsible usage, and an understanding of its impact to harness its full potential.

HIGHLIGHTING KEY TRENDS AND EMERGING PLATFORMS IN THE SOCIAL MEDIA LANDSCAPE.

The social media landscape is ever-evolving, with new trends and platforms constantly emerging. Staying abreast of these developments is crucial for businesses and individuals seeking to maximize their reach and engagement. In this section, we will highlight some key trends and emerging platforms that are shaping the social media landscape and explain why they are significant.

Video Content Dominance: Video has become the dominant form of content across social media platforms. Short-form videos, such as those found on TikTok and Instagram Reels, have gained immense popularity due to their ability to entertain, inform, and capture attention in a short span of time. The rise of video content reflects the shift in consumer preferences towards immersive and visually engaging experiences.

Live Streaming: Live streaming has experienced exponential growth, allowing businesses and individuals to connect with their audience in real-time. Platforms like Facebook Live, Instagram Live, and YouTube Live enable instant engagement, fostering authentic and interactive connections. Live streaming is particularly effective for product launches, behind-the-scenes glimpses, and hosting virtual events.

Ephemeral Content: Ephemeral content, which disappears after a certain period, has gained traction with platforms like Snapchat and Instagram Stories. This trend capitalizes on the fear of missing out (FOMO) and encourages users to engage with content quickly. Ephemeral content offers a sense of authenticity and spontaneity, fostering a deeper connection between brands and their audience.

Social Commerce: The integration of e-commerce within social media platforms has transformed the way businesses sell products. Features like Instagram Shopping, Facebook Shops, and Pinterest's Shopping Pins allow users to discover and purchase products seamlessly within their social media feeds. This trend eliminates the need for users to navigate away from the platform, streamlining the purchasing process.

Influencer Marketing and User-Generated Content: Influencer marketing continues to play a significant role in social media, as influencers have the ability to influence purchasing decisions and engage large audiences. Additionally, user-generated content (UGC) has become a powerful tool for brands, as it enhances authenticity and encourages user participation, fostering a sense of community and brand advocacy.

Emerging Platforms

Facebook: This remains one of the largest and most influential social media platforms, connecting billions of users worldwide. It offers a diverse range of features for individuals and businesses, including personal profiles, business pages, groups, and advertising opportunities. Facebook continues to adapt by integrating features such as Facebook Live,

Stories, and Marketplace to cater to changing user behaviors and expectations.

Instagram: This isowned by Facebook, has experienced tremendous growth in recent years, particularly among younger demographics. Known for its visual storytelling capabilities, Instagram offers a highly engaging platform for sharing photos, videos, and Stories. With the introduction of features like Reels and IGTV, Instagram has expanded its reach and provided new opportunities for creators, influencers, and businesses to captivate audiences and drive engagement.

Twitter: Also known for its real-time microblogging format, has established itself as a prominent platform for news, conversations, and trends. Its character-limited posts, known as tweets, enable users to share thoughts, news updates, and engage in public discussions. Twitter's unique features, such as hashtags and retweets, have made it a powerful tool for amplifying messages, sparking conversations, and connecting with a global audience.

Clubhouse: Clubhouse is an audio-based social networking app that gained popularity for its exclusive and real-time conversations. It allows users to join rooms and participate in discussions on various topics. Clubhouse has created a new space for networking, knowledge sharing, and community-building through audio interactions.

TikTok: TikTok has rapidly become a global sensation, particularly among younger demographics. Its short-form video format, creative editing tools, and algorithm-driven content discovery have fueled its success. TikTok offers businesses and creators an opportunity to reach a massive and highly engaged audience with innovative and viral content.

These trends and emerging platforms are significant because they represent the changing dynamics of user preferences, content consumption, and brand-consumer interactions. They provide new avenues for businesses to connect with their target audience, enhance brand visibility, and drive engagement. By embracing these trends and leveraging emerging platforms, businesses and individuals can stay ahead of the curve and maximize their impact in the evolving social media landscape.

Chapter Three

BUILDING THE FOUNDATION

Understanding the role of strategies in social media management.

Content creation

Content creation is a fundamental aspect of social media management that involves developing and sharing valuable, relevant, and engaging content to attract and retain an audience. It plays a pivotal role in establishing a strong online presence, building brand awareness, and driving audience engagement. To make content creation positive result orienting, it's essential to follow a systematic approach and consider the following key aspects:

Define Your Target Audience: Start by understanding your target audience, their demographics, interests, and pain points. This knowledge will guide you in creating content that resonates with them and meets their needs.

Set Clear Objectives: Determine your content objectives, whether it's to increase brand visibility, drive website traffic, generate leads, or educate your audience. Clear objectives will help you align your content creation efforts with your overall marketing goals.

Research and Ideation: Conduct research to identify popular topics, industry trends, and keywords relevant to your audience. Use tools like keyword planners, social media listening, and competitor analysis to generate ideas for your content.

Develop a Content Calendar: Create a content calendar to plan and organize your content creation process. It ensures consistency and helps you stay on track with your content strategy. Allocate specific time slots for brainstorming, creating, and scheduling your content.

Create Compelling and Valuable Content: Craft content that provides value to your audience. Focus on creating informative, educational, entertaining, or inspiring content that aligns with your brand's voice and resonates with your target audience.

Utilize Different Content Formats: Diversify your content by leveraging various formats such as blog articles, videos, infographics, podcasts, or live streams, images that are not copyrighted,and behind the scene images (BTS).

Different formats cater to different preferences and can help you reach a broader audience.

Optimize for Search Engines and Social Media: Incorporate relevant keywords, meta tags, and descriptions to optimize your content for search engines. Additionally, ensure your content is shareable by adding social media buttons, engaging visuals, and compelling headlines.

Engage with Your Audience: Actively respond to comments, messages, and mentions from your audience. Encourage discussions, ask questions, and foster a sense of community around your content. Engaging with your audience builds trust and strengthens your online presence.

Analyze and Iterate: Regularly track and analyze the performance of your content using social media analytics and website analytics tools. Identify what works well and what needs improvement, and adjust your content creation strategy accordingly.

Stay Updated and Evolve: Keep up with the latest industry trends, algorithm changes, and audience preferences. Continuously learn and adapt your content creation strategy to stay relevant and maintain audience engagement.

How to use ChatGPT to generate ideas for your content

Understanding ChatGPT

ChatGPT is an AI language model designed to generate human-like text responses. It can assist users in generating content, answering questions, and providing suggestions. It's important to note that ChatGPT operates based on patterns and examples from the training data it has been exposed to, so it may not always provide perfect responses. Ensure to sign up so you can have an account to start your journey. Log on to chat.openai.com

Framing the Query: When using ChatGPT, it's crucial to frame your queries or prompts clearly and precisely. State your request or question in a way that provides the necessary context and details for ChatGPT to generate a relevant response. Be specific and avoid ambiguous or open-ended queries.

Example

Hello, please I want to make a calendar for my next month social media management but am short of ideas. Can you please help me with good ideas and possible ways I can implement them in my calendar?

Experiment and Refine: ChatGPT's responses may vary depending on the input provided. It's recommended to experiment with different phrasing, rephrase questions, or modify the context to obtain desired results. If the initial response doesn't meet your expectations, consider refining the input or trying alternative approaches.

Iterative Feedback: ChatGPT can be guided and improved through iterative feedback. If the generated response is not accurate or satisfactory, users can provide explicit feedback by specifying what was incorrect or requesting a different response. This feedback helps fine-tune the model and improve its performance over time.

Contextual Prompts: To enhance the quality of responses, provide relevant context in your prompts. You can share relevant details, specify the desired tone or style, or mention any constraints or requirements. This helps ChatGPT better understand the specific intent and generate more tailored responses.

Evaluate and Review: It's important to evaluate the responses generated by ChatGPT critically. While it can provide useful insights and suggestions, it's essential to review the output for accuracy, coherence, and alignment with your specific goals and brand voice. Use your judgment to determine which suggestions or responses are most suitable for your social media management strategy.

Ethical Use and Considerations: When using ChatGPT, it's crucial to prioritize ethical considerations. Avoid using the model to generate misleading or false information, engage in harmful activities, or impersonate individuals or organizations. Use ChatGPT responsibly and ensure the content aligns with ethical guidelines and legal requirements.

Stay Up to Date: Keep in mind that ChatGPT is an evolving technology, and updates may be released to enhance its capabilities. Stay informed about the latest developments, improvements, and any guidelines provided by OpenAI or the platform you are using to access ChatGPT.

NOTE:

This AI tool is not meant to replace your research ability or cause laziness or dependency, rather its to help you with ideas you can develop to have a beautiful content.

Copywriting

Copywriting is the art of crafting persuasive and compelling written content with the goal of influencing the reader to take a desired action. It is a skill that can be implemented effectively by following these key principles:

Know Your Audience: Understand your target audience's needs, desires, and pain points. Tailor your copy to resonate with them, using language and tone that speaks directly to their motivations and interests.

Focus on Benefits: Highlight the benefits and value your product or service offers. Instead of just listing features, explain how it solves a problem or improves the customer's life. Show them the positive impact it can have.

Write Clear and Concise Headlines: Capture attention with powerful, attention-grabbing headlines. Clearly convey the main benefit or offer to entice the reader to continue reading. Keep it concise, yet compelling.

Use Persuasive Language: Use persuasive language and storytelling techniques to engage and captivate your audience. Emphasize the emotional appeal of your product or service, and demonstrate how it can fulfill their desires or solve their problems.

Create a Sense of Urgency: Encourage immediate action by creating a sense of urgency. Highlight limited-time offers, exclusive deals, or scarcity to motivate the reader to act promptly.

Include Social Proof: Incorporate testimonials, reviews, and case studies to build trust and credibility. People are more likely to be convinced when they see others benefiting from your product or service.

Craft a Strong Call-to-Action (CTA): Clearly direct your readers on what action to take next. Make your CTA specific, compelling, and easy to follow. Use action-oriented words that encourage immediate response.

Edit and Proofread: Ensure your copy is free of errors, grammatical mistakes, and typos. Edit your content to improve clarity and readability. A polished, error-free copy enhances your credibility and professionalism.

Test and Iterate: Continuously test different copy variations to identify what resonates best with your audience. Monitor and analyze the performance of your copy, making adjustments based on data-driven insights.

Practice Empathy: Put yourself in the shoes of your audience and write from their perspective. Understand their challenges, aspirations, and concerns. Show empathy in your copy to connect on a deeper level.

By implementing these principles, you can enhance your copywriting skills and create persuasive, impactful content that resonates with your target audience. Remember to adapt your approach based on audience feedback and constantly refine your copy to improve results.

Content publishing

Content publishing is a critical aspect of a successful social media management strategy. It involves the process of distributing and sharing your content across various platforms to reach your target audience. Implementing effective content publishing practices can maximize the visibility and impact of your content. Here are key considerations to help you during implementation:

Consistent Brand Voice: Maintain a consistent brand voice across all your content. This ensures that your messaging aligns with your brand identity and values. Develop guidelines for tone, style, and language to create a cohesive brand experience.

Content Calendar: Create a content calendar to plan and organize your publishing schedule. It helps you stay organized, ensures consistent content flow, and prevents last-minute scrambling. Include important dates, events, and campaigns to align your content with relevant occasions.

Optimal Timing: Identify the optimal times to publish your content based on your audience's online behavior and platform analytics. Experiment with different publishing times and analyze engagement metrics to determine the most effective timing for reaching your target audience.

Platform-Specific Optimization: Customize your content for each social media platform. Understand the unique features and user behavior of each platform and optimize your content accordingly. For example, use hashtags on Instagram and Twitter, optimize descriptions for search on YouTube, and utilize LinkedIn's professional tone.

Visual Appeal: Incorporate visually appealing elements into your content. Use high-quality images, videos, info graphics, and other visual formats to capture attention and enhance engagement.

Optimize visuals for each platform to ensure they display properly and attractively.

Engage with Your Audience: Publishing content is not a one-way street. Actively engage with your audience by responding to comments, messages, and mentions. Encourage conversation, ask questions, and build relationships. Engaging with your audience fosters loyalty and creates a sense of community.

Analyze Performance: Regularly analyze the performance of your published content using platform analytics and other monitoring tools. Track metrics such as reach, engagement, click-through rates, and conversions. This data provides insights into what content resonates best with your audience and informs future publishing decisions.

Experiment and Iterate: Don't be afraid to experiment with different content formats, topics, and approaches. Monitor the results and iterate based on audience feedback. Continuously optimize and improve your content publishing strategy to achieve better outcomes.

Repurpose and Recycle Content: Maximize the value of your content by repurposing it across different platforms and formats. For example, turn a blog post into a video or create social media snippets from a podcast episode. Recycling content allows you to reach new audiences and extend the lifespan of your content.

Stay Relevant and Up-to-Date: Keep a finger on the pulse of industry trends, platform updates, and audience preferences. Stay informed about changes in algorithms, new features, and emerging platforms. Adapting your content publishing strategy to align with these changes helps you stay relevant and maintain audience engagement.

By implementing these content publishing practices, you can effectively distribute your content, increase its visibility, and engage with your target audience. Consistency, optimization, engagement, and continuous improvement are key to successful content publishing and achieving your social media goals.

Exploring target audience, and the use of key performance indicators (KPIs)

The target audience refers to the specific group of people who a brand intends to reach with its marketing messages and offerings. It is a defined segment of the population with shared characteristics, behaviors, and preferences. Identifying the target audience is crucial as it allows brands to tailor their marketing efforts and create messages that resonate with the intended recipients. Understanding the target audience helps brands allocate resources effectively, deliver relevant content, and build meaningful connections. It involves analyzing demographic, psychographic, and behavioral attributes to gain insights into the audience's characteristics and interests. Ultimately, defining the target audience helps brands maximize the impact of their marketing strategies and achieve desired business outcomes.

Understanding your target audience is paramount in social media management as it forms the foundation for creating engaging and relevant content, driving meaningful interactions, and achieving your business objectives. Here are key reasons why targeting the right audience is crucial:

Relevance and Personalization: By knowing your target audience, you can create content that resonates with their interests, preferences, and pain points. This level of relevance and personalization increases the chances of capturing their attention, fostering a connection, and driving engagement.

Precise Messaging: Different audience segments have distinct needs, motivations, and communication styles. When you understand your target audience, you can craft messages that address their specific concerns and aspirations. Tailored messaging establishes credibility, builds trust, and increases the likelihood of achieving desired outcomes.

Efficient Resource Allocation: Knowing your target audience helps optimize your resources, including time, budget, and effort. By focusing your efforts on reaching the right people, you can avoid wasting resources on irrelevant audiences. This allows you to maximize the impact of your social media campaigns and deliver measurable results.

Enhanced Customer Insights: Understanding your target audience goes beyond demographics. It involves gaining deep insights into their behaviors, preferences, and decision-making processes. This knowledge empowers you to make data-driven decisions, refine your social media strategy, and continuously improve your engagement with the audience.

Effective Advertising: Social media platforms provide powerful advertising tools that allow you to target specific audience segments based on demographics, interests, and behaviors. When you have a clear understanding of your target audience, you can leverage these tools to deliver highly targeted ads, maximizing their impact and improving return on investment (ROI).

Community Building: Building a strong community of loyal followers is a key objective for many brands. When you know your target audience, you can foster a sense of belonging and create a community where individuals feel understood and valued. This cultivates brand advocacy, word-of-mouth marketing, and long-term customer loyalty.

To identify and understand your target audience effectively, conduct market research, analyze customer data, and engage in social listening. Utilize tools and analytics provided by social media platforms to gain insights into audience demographics, engagement metrics, and content performance. Regularly monitor and adapt your strategy based on audience feedback and evolving market trends.

By prioritizing your target audience in social media management, you can build meaningful connections, drive engagement, and ultimately achieve your business goals.

Here are some examples of target audiences and the types of brands they can be relevant for across various industries:

Fitness Enthusiasts and Health Conscious Individuals

Brands: Athletic apparel companies, fitness equipment manufacturers, health supplement brands, fitness apps.

Tech-savvy Millennials and Gen Z

Brands: Smartphone manufacturers, app developers, social media platforms, streaming services, tech accessories.

Foodies and Culinary Enthusiasts

Brands: Gourmet food brands, cooking utensil manufacturers, culinary schools, food delivery services, recipe blogs.

Travelers and Adventure Seekers

Brands: Airlines, travel agencies, outdoor gear companies, adventure tourism operators, hotel chains.

Parents and Families

Brands: Baby product manufacturers, educational toy companies, family-friendly entertainment venues, parenting blogs.

Fashionistas and Style Influencers

Brands: Fashion designers, clothing retailers, luxury brands, beauty and cosmetics companies, fashion magazines.

Business Professionals and Entrepreneurs

Brands: Business coaching services, productivity apps, professional networking platforms, office supply companies.

Pet Lovers and Animal Welfare Advocates

Brands: Pet food manufacturers, pet care services, animal shelters, veterinary clinics, pet accessory brands.

Environmentalists and Sustainability Advocates

Brands: Eco-friendly product companies, renewable energy providers, sustainable fashion brands, conservation organizations.

Art and Culture Enthusiasts

Brands: Art galleries, museums, music festivals, publishing houses, art supply stores, theater production companies.

Remember, these are just examples to illustrate the variety of target audiences and industries. The actual target audience for a specific brand will depend on factors such as the nature of the product/service, brand values, and the industry it operates in. It's essential to conduct market research and understand the unique characteristics and preferences of your target audience to effectively tailor your brand's messaging and offerings.

The use of KPIs and metrics

The use of Key Performance Indicators (KPIs) and metrics is essential in social media management to measure the effectiveness of strategies, track progress towards goals, and make data-driven decisions. Here's a discussion on the importance and use of KPIs and metrics in social media management:

Setting Clear Objectives: Before determining which KPIs and metrics to track, it's crucial to establish clear objectives for your social media efforts. These objectives could include increasing brand awareness, driving website traffic, generating leads, or improving customer engagement. Clear objectives help align KPIs and metrics with specific goals.

Choosing Relevant KPIs: KPIs are specific performance indicators that reflect progress towards achieving objectives. The choice of KPIs depends on your objectives and can include metrics such as reach, engagement rate, click-through rate, conversion rate, follower growth, and sentiment analysis. Select KPIs that align with your goals and provide meaningful insights into your social media performance.

Measuring Reach and Engagement: Reach metrics, such as the number of impressions or followers, indicate the size of your social media audience. Engagement metrics, such as likes, comments, shares, and click-throughs, measure the level of interaction and interest generated by your content. These metrics help gauge the effectiveness of your messaging and content strategy.

Tracking Conversion Metrics: Conversion metrics assess the impact of social media efforts on desired actions, such as website conversions, lead generation, or sales. Metrics like conversion rate, cost per conversion, and revenue generated from social media channels provide insights into the return on investment (ROI) and effectiveness of your social media campaigns.

Monitoring Customer Sentiment: Social media platforms offer valuable insights into customer sentiment through metrics like sentiment analysis and social listening. Monitoring sentiment helps you understand how customers perceive your brand, identify areas for improvement, and respond to customer feedback and concerns promptly.

Analyzing Audience Demographics: Social media platforms provide demographic data about your audience, such as age, gender, location, and interests. Analyzing these metrics helps tailor your content, messaging, and targeting to better reach and engage your target audience.

Benchmarking and Competitor Analysis: Benchmarking your social media performance against industry standards and competitors' metrics provides valuable insights. Comparing metrics like engagement rates, follower growth, and content performance can help identify areas of improvement, uncover industry trends, and refine your social media strategy.

Regular Reporting and Analysis: Regularly track, analyze, and report on your social media metrics. Use social media analytics tools and platforms to gather data, visualize trends, and gain actionable insights. Regular analysis helps identify patterns, measure progress, and make informed decisions to optimize your social media management efforts.

Iterative Optimization: Use the data and insights from your KPIs and metrics to refine your social media strategy. Identify areas of improvement, experiment with different content formats, messaging, or targeting approaches, and measure the impact of changes based on the tracked metrics. Continuously optimize your social media management efforts based on data-driven insights.

By using relevant KPIs and metrics in social media management, you can measure the effectiveness of your strategies, identify areas for improvement, and make informed decisions to drive better results. It allows you to track progress, demonstrate ROI, and align your social media efforts with your overall business objectives.

SECTION TWO

IMPLEMENTING THE GOALS AND OBJECTIVES
OF SOCIAL MEDIA MANAGEMENT

Chapter Four

GROWING SOCIAL MEDIA FOLLOWERS BY

Increasing brand awareness

Growing a social media account involves increasing brand awareness, which can be achieved through several key strategies. First, define your brand identity and create a consistent content strategy that aligns with your target audience. Optimize your profiles for discoverability and leverage compelling visual content to capture attention. Engage with your audience, collaborate with influencers, and run targeted advertising campaigns to expand your reach. Harness user-generated content, monitor analytics, and adjust strategies accordingly. By implementing these tactics consistently, you can successfully grow your social media account and increase brand awareness.

Collaboration method

Growing a social media account through collaboration involves partnering with influencers, industry experts, or complementary brands to expand your reach and increase brand awareness. By collaborating with others, you tap into their existing audience and benefit from their credibility and influence. Identify relevant collaborators, establish mutually beneficial partnerships, and leverage their platforms to promote your brand. Through collaborative efforts, you can access new audiences, gain exposure, and build relationships within the social media community, ultimately driving the growth of your account and increasing brand awareness.

Contest

Growing a social media account through contests is an effective strategy to increase engagement and attract new followers. Create engaging and shareable contest mechanics, such as liking, commenting, or sharing content to enter. Offer appealing prizes that align with your brand and target audience's interests. Promote the contest through social media posts, paid advertising, and collaborations with influencers. Encourage participants to tag friends and share your content, thereby expanding your reach organically. Leverage the contest to collect user-generated content and build a sense of community. By running well-executed contests, you can drive engagement, gain followers, and enhance brand awareness on social media.

Hash tags and mentions.

Hashtags and mentions are valuable tools in social media marketing that can help increase reach, engagement, and brand visibility. Here's a discussion on their use and how to effectively leverage them:

Hashtags:

Use of Hashtags: Hashtags categorize content and make it discoverable to a wider audience. They help users find relevant posts and topics of interest.

Research Trending Hashtags: Research and identify popular and relevant hashtags in your industry or niche. Use tools like hashtag generators or explore trending topics on social media platforms.

Be Specific and Relevant: Use hashtags that are specific to your content and align with your target audience's interests. Avoid using generic or overused hashtags that may not attract the right audience.

Don't Overdo It: Use a limited number of hashtags (2-5) per post. Focus on quality rather than quantity, and ensure they are relevant to your content.

Mentions:

Use of Mentions: Mentions involve tagging or mentioning other social media users in your posts or comments. This can help increase engagement, foster relationships, and collaborate with others.

Engage with Influencers and Partners: Mention relevant influencers, industry experts, or partner brands in your posts to get their attention, build relationships, and potentially attract their followers.

Encourage User-generated Content: Prompt your audience to mention your brand in their posts by running contests, campaigns, or asking for feedback. This generates user-generated content and expands your reach.

Respond and Acknowledge Mentions: Monitor your mentions regularly and respond promptly. Acknowledge and engage with users who mention your brand, as this fosters a positive relationship and encourages further interactions.

When using hashtags and mentions, it's important to follow best practices:

Research and select hashtags and mentions that align with your brand and target audience.

Monitor and engage with posts using your chosen hashtags and mentions to join relevant conversations.

Track the performance of your posts using specific hashtags and mentions to understand their impact and adjust your strategy if needed.

Remember, hashtags and mentions are not only about gaining visibility but also about building connections and engaging with your audience. Use them strategically and thoughtfully to enhance your social media presence and foster meaningful interactions.

Here are some examples of popular and commonly used hashtags across different industries and interests:

#Travelgram: Used by travel enthusiasts and influencers to share captivating travel photos and experiences.

#Foodie: A hashtag used by food lovers to share delicious food pictures, restaurant recommendations, and recipes.

#FitnessMotivation: Fitness enthusiasts use this hashtag to share workout routines, fitness tips, and progress updates.

#FashionInspiration: Fashion influencers and brands use this hashtag to showcase stylish outfits, fashion trends, and outfit inspirations.

#MondayMotivation: A hashtag used to kickstart the week with inspirational quotes, positive affirmations, and motivating messages.

#ThrowbackThursday (#TBT): A popular hashtag used on Thursdays to share nostalgic photos or memories from the past.

#DigitalMarketing: Used by professionals and businesses in the digital marketing industry to discuss strategies, trends, and insights related to online marketing.

#SelfCareSunday: A hashtag associated with self-care practices, where individuals share their wellness routines, relaxation tips, and self-care rituals.

#PetsOfInstagram: Pet owners use this hashtag to showcase adorable pictures of their pets and connect with fellow animal lovers.

#MondayMood: A hashtag used to express different emotions or moods on Mondays, reflecting the start of a new week.

Remember to research industry-specific hashtags relevant to your brand and target audience. The examples above provide a starting point, but it's important to identify hashtags that are specific to your niche and resonate with your target audience.

y to discuss strategies, trends, and insights related to online marketing.

#SelfCareSunday: A hashtag associated with self-care practices, where individuals share their wellness routines, relaxation tips, and self-care rituals.

#PetsOfInstagram: Pet owners use this hashtag to showcase adorable pictures of their pets and connect with fellow animal lovers.

#MondayMood: A hashtag used to express different emotions or moods on Mondays, reflecting the start of a new week.

Remember to research industry-specific hashtags relevant to your brand and target audience. The examples above provide a starting point, but it's important to identify hashtags that are specific to your niche and resonate with your target audience.

SECTION

THREE

THE USE OF ADVERTISEMENT

Chapter Five

FACE BOOK AND INSTAGRAM ADS

Using brand awareness objective

The primary objective of Facebook ads for brand awareness is to increase the visibility and recognition of a brand among the target audience. Here's a summary of the key aspects of brand awareness objectives in Facebook ads:

Reach and Impressions: The focus is on maximizing the number of unique users who see the ad (reach) and the total number of times the ad is displayed (impressions). This helps to expose the brand to a wider audience and increase its overall visibility.

Ad Placement: Strategic ad placement ensures that the ads are shown in prominent positions within the Facebook platform, such as in the news feed or right-hand column, to capture users' attention effectively.

Engaging Ad Creative: Compelling and visually appealing ad creatives, including images, videos, or carousels, are used to grab the attention of users as they scroll through their feed. The goal is to leave a lasting impression and generate interest in the brand.

Brand Consistency: Consistent branding elements, such as logos, colors, and messaging, are incorporated into the ad creative to reinforce brand identity and improve brand recall.

Frequency Control: Managing the frequency of ad impressions helps prevent ad fatigue and ensures that users see the brand's message enough times to make an impact without overwhelming them.

Ad Recall and Brand Lift Studies: Facebook provides tools to measure ad recall and brand lift, allowing advertisers to assess the impact of their brand awareness campaigns and make data-driven optimizations.

By setting clear brand awareness objectives, utilizing engaging ad creatives, targeting the right audience, and tracking key metrics, advertisers can effectively leverage Facebook ads to enhance brand recognition and increase brand awareness among their target audience.

Using traffic objective

The traffic objective in Facebook ads aims to drive more traffic to a website, landing page, or specific destination. Here's a summary of the key elements involved in the traffic objective:

Link Clicks: The primary goal is to generate clicks on the ad's call-to-action button, directing users to the desired destination.

Ad Creative: Attention-grabbing visuals and compelling ad copy are used to entice users to click on the ad and explore the offered content or offer.

Targeting: Specific targeting options such as demographics, interests, behaviors, and custom audiences are utilized to reach the right audience who are more likely to engage with the ad and click through to the destination.

Ad Placement: Ads are strategically placed in locations where they are likely to receive high visibility, such as the Facebook news feed, Instagram feed, or in-stream videos.

Call-to-Action (CTA) Button: The ad includes a prominent CTA button that encourages users to take action, such as "Learn More," "Shop Now," or "Sign Up," making it clear and compelling for users to click.

Landing Page Optimization: The destination page should be well-optimized, providing a seamless user experience, relevant information, and a clear path for users to take the desired action.

Conversion Tracking: Facebook's tracking pixel or other conversion tracking methods are implemented to measure and analyze the effectiveness of the traffic campaign, helping optimize targeting and ad performance.

By setting clear traffic objectives, using compelling ad creatives, targeting the right audience, and optimizing the destination page, businesses can effectively drive traffic from Facebook ads to their desired destination, increasing website visits, lead generation, or other desired actions.

Using lead objective

The lead objective in Facebook ads allows businesses to capture valuable user information and generate leads directly on the platform. Here's a summary of how the lead objective is used in Facebook ads:

Capturing User Information: With the lead objective, businesses can create lead forms within the ad, enabling users to submit their contact details without leaving Facebook.

Generating High-Quality Leads: By using lead forms, businesses can attract users who are genuinely interested in their products or services, resulting in higher-quality leads.

Simplifying the User Experience: Lead forms streamline the lead generation process by eliminating the need for users to navigate to an external website or fill out lengthy forms.

Customizable Form Fields: The lead forms can be customized to collect specific information relevant to the business, such as name, email address, phone number, or other details required for lead qualification.

Incentivizing User Action: To encourage users to provide their information, businesses can offer incentives such as exclusive content, discounts, or access to special promotions.

Efficient Lead Management: Facebook provides tools to manage and download the captured lead data, making it easier for businesses to follow up and nurture leads effectively.

Integration and Automation: The lead data can be integrated with CRM systems or other marketing tools, allowing businesses to automate lead nurturing processes and enhance lead management efficiency.

Measuring and Optimizing Performance: Facebook's conversion tracking tools enable businesses to measure the performance of lead campaigns, including metrics like cost per lead and conversion rate. This data can be used to optimize targeting and ad strategies for better results.

By leveraging the lead objective in Facebook ads, businesses can efficiently capture user information, generate high-quality leads, and streamline the lead generation process, ultimately driving growth and conversions for their business.

Twitter influencing

Twitter influencing by influencers plays a significant role in social media management, contributing to brand visibility, engagement, and overall online presence. Here's a discussion on how Twitter influencers can positively impact social media management:

Increased Reach and Exposure: Influencers on Twitter have established a dedicated following, often consisting of individuals interested in specific niches or industries. By partnering with influencers, brands can tap into their audience and benefit from increased reach, exposing their message to a wider range of users.

Authenticity and Credibility: Twitter influencers have built trust and credibility with their followers through consistent and valuable content. When influencers endorse a brand or product, their followers perceive it as a genuine recommendation, leading to higher trust and potential conversions.

Engaging and Interactive Content: Influencers excel at creating engaging and interactive content that resonates with their audience. By collaborating with influencers, brands can leverage their creativity and expertise to develop compelling Twitter campaigns, including live chats, Q&A sessions, polls, and contests, fostering higher user engagement and interaction.

Trend Amplification: Influencers are often early adopters of trends and have a pulse on the latest news and developments. When they engage with trending topics on Twitter, their influence can help amplify the reach and visibility of brand-related content, increasing brand awareness and driving conversations.

Targeted Audience Segmentation: Influencers on Twitter often have a well-defined target audience based on their niche or expertise. This allows brands to align their marketing efforts with influencers who have followers matching their desired target audience, ensuring their message reaches the right people.

Social Proof and User-generated Content: Influencers' endorsements and mentions can serve as social proof, influencing their followers to explore and engage with the brand. Additionally, user-generated content resulting from influencer collaborations can provide valuable content assets for brands to leverage in their social media management strategy.

Data-driven Insights: Influencer collaborations on Twitter can provide brands with valuable data and insights. By tracking engagement, sentiment, and other metrics, brands can gain a deeper understanding of their target audience, preferences, and the impact of their influencer partnerships.

Relationship Building: Collaborating with influencers on Twitter fosters long-term relationships with individuals who can serve as brand advocates. These relationships can extend beyond a single campaign, leading to ongoing partnerships and a network of influencers supporting the brand's social media efforts.

Twitter influencers play a vital role in social media management by extending brand reach, enhancing awareness, credibility, fostering engagement, and providing valuable insights. Partnering with influencers allows brands to tap into their expertise and audience, resulting in increased brand awareness, improved online presence, and ultimately driving business growth.

LinkedIn building

Building a strong presence on LinkedIn is crucial for professionals and businesses looking to network, establish thought leadership, and create valuable connections. Here's a discussion on what to do and what not to do when building your LinkedIn profile and engaging on the platform:

What to Do on LinkedIn:

Optimize Your Profile: Create a comprehensive and professional LinkedIn profile. Include a clear and engaging headline, a well-written summary, relevant work experience, skills, and education. Use keywords to enhance visibility in searches.

Showcase Your Expertise: Share valuable content related to your industry or area of expertise. Publish articles, share industry insights, and engage in thoughtful discussions to establish yourself as a thought leader and provide value to your connections.

Engage and Network: Actively engage with others by commenting on their posts, joining relevant groups, and participating in discussions. Build meaningful connections by reaching out to professionals you admire or have common interests with.

Personalize Connection Requests: When sending connection requests, personalize the message. Explain why you want to connect and how you can add value to each other's professional networks. Avoid sending generic or spammy connection requests.

Go fork Recommendations and Endorsements: Request recommendations from colleagues, clients, or supervisors to build credibility. Seek endorsements for your skills to highlight your expertise. Provide genuine recommendations and endorsements for others as well.

What Not to Do on LinkedIn:

Don't Be too Promotional: While it's important to showcase your achievements, avoid being too promotional or constantly selling your products or services. Focus on providing valuable content like motivational and problem solving contents and building relationships, rather than a constant sales pitch.

Avoid Incomplete or Inconsistent Profiles: Ensure your LinkedIn profile is complete, up-to-date, and consistent with your professional brand. Incomplete or inconsistent profiles can give a negative impression and hinder your networking efforts.

Avoid engaging in Controversial Discussions: Maintain professionalism and avoid engaging in negative or controversial discussions that can harm your reputation. Stay positive, respectful, and focus on constructive conversations.

Avoid Sending Irrelevant Messages: Respect others' privacy and avoid spamming or sending unsolicited messages. Personalize your messages and ensure they are relevant to the recipient's professional interests.

Do not Neglect LinkedIn: Consistency is key on LinkedIn. Don't create a profile and then neglect it.

Regularly update your profile, engage with your connections, and stay active in relevant groups and discussions to maximize your presence and networking opportunities.

Building your LinkedIn profile and engaging on the platform requires a strategic approach. By implementing these best practices and avoiding common pitfalls, you can effectively build your professional network, establish credibility, and leverage LinkedIn's vast opportunities for career growth and business success as well.

www.ingramcontent.com/pod-product-compliance
Lightning Source LLC
Chambersburg PA
CBHW062342290526
45794CB00005B/2077